LOSS IS A DOOR

ABDULKAREEM ABDULKAREEM

Published by Akashic Books

ISBN: 978-1-63614-250-0

Printed in China
First printing

EU Authorized Representative details:
Easy Access System Europe
Mustamäe tee 50, 10621 Tallinn, Estonia
gpsr.request@easproject.com

Akashic Books
Instagram, X, Facebook: AkashicBooks
info@akashicbooks.com
www.akashicbooks.com

African Poetry Book Fund
Brown University
10 Prospect Street
Box A
Providence, RI 02912

For my dad, Abdulfatah Abdulkareem

TABLE OF CONTENTS

PREFACE

by Saddiq Dzukogi

Loss Is a Door is a literary door to the mind of a poet devoted to the spiritual, communal, abstract, and concrete, as well as to the sequences of sound and music that help us make sense of the lyric's contours. Here we encounter poetry of rich description, dazzling imagery, and rhythms both flowing and abrupt. Music bridges the gap between clarity and ambiguity, such that no meaning feels lost, even in moments when we stand outside language. Abdulkareem Abdulkareem's spiritual and cultural identities as a Yoruba Muslim are mostly not in conflict, and when they are, the conflict leads to further self-grounding and discovery.

Abdulkareem is conscious of the social and spiritual in equal measure. In the poem "Black River," he takes on the environmental damage that oil exploration in the southern region of Nigeria has brought to the residents of Port Harcourt. With language and imagery that are lucid and sometimes unsettling, the poem is a harrowing depiction of environmental and human suffering caused by ecological degradation and the devastating impact of oil pollution. The poet employs the use of consonant sounds and dissonant combinations to evoke the harshness of the environment:

> My mother stands motionless in the water,
> infested by oil, drowned in half—her black-colored
>
> palms clasped together, whispering the
> language creamed w/ oil. We greet mornings from the height
>
> of our raft & wake to sooty breakfasts
> with breaths of carbon.

The recurrent use of strong *c* sounds, as in "clasped," "creamed," and "black-colored," generates a staccato effect that heightens the feeling of grimness and unease. This jarring pattern is further enhanced by the pacing of the lines, emphasizing the abrupt and often violent changes in the lives of Port Harcourt residents. Abdulkareem continues, "My uncle became breathless / upholding convulsion in the terra incognita / of his body" ("Black River"). Here, as elsewhere throughout the collection, Abdulkareem writes with empathy and lamentation even as he explores a historical moment. The poet functions as observer, storyteller, and reporter, all without losing the music of genuine lyricism:

The woman at the edge

of the interview holds on to her tears—
          says: *I came to the camp handful with my son, but I'm leaving*

   with hands empty of him—again, *I know the past belongs*
      in the past, my son belonged to the past, but my grievances

belong to the future. The footbridge collapsed,
      see how water beholds teeth.

("Black River")

In the poem "Eid al-Fitr in Ilorin," we witness a poet in the midst of spiritual renewal, investigating the relationship between tradition and personal meditation. Eid is presented as a moment of both outward celebration and inward contemplation, blending religious devotion with the personal experience of pilgrimage and prayer:

Again, the morning comes alive like a season
of harvest, of prayers. I unmask the day,
my mouth cascading clean waterfall with a bright-eyed
smile. Holiness dawns on me—& I
unbottle a single alhamdulillah like a fine stereo.

The language portrays the sense of virtue and delight associated with the festival. The comparison of a prayer of thanks to the sound of a "fine stereo" emphasizes the clarity and resonance of this spiritual gratitude. The poem is reverent and celebratory, with a strong sense of communal pride and spiritual fulfillment.

Throughout the collection, however, Abdulkareem Abdulkareem builds another world: one of despair, existential angst, and questioning. The poem "In Another World of Living" creates a stark contrast between an idealized vision of happiness and the harsh reality of loneliness: "fire dies in your throat / a god relinquishing the light of what you seek." The image of fire dying in the throat hints at a loss of passion or hope, while "god relinquishing . . . light" suggests a loss of divine guidance. Abdulkareem continues, "jubilance eludes you / in every universe / you an alien in a world of elation." These lines demonstrate a profound sense of alienation and inability to find joy or belonging, reinforcing the isolation experienced in the search for meaning.

In "Intersections," Abdulkareem writes, "How the use of language can become a sacrilege / deep in the fiber of tongues." In a nuanced and contemplative manner, the poem explores the complexities of language and its role in affecting identity and belief. This examination of language—its duality as both a unifying and disruptive force—is exquisite.

Another poem that exemplifies Abdulkareem's facility with language, sound, and symbolism is "Confabulation," an emotionally resonant poem that explores the convolution of memory and desire.

The poet grapples with the tension between his longing for concrete memories and the ephemeral, often elusive nature of what is actually remembered. The term "confabulation" denotes the creation of distorted memories, serving as a potent lens through which the poet examines the fragility and unreliability of his recollections. In this poem, as across the whole collection, the use of symbolism ("Forgetfulness, like effigies in the dark") is palpable.

Loss Is a Door is a remarkable book: part worship, part grief. It forms a poetic procession into a world that may seem familiar, one that demands attention to cultural, spiritual, and deeply personal landscapes, both lived and imagined. Abdulkareem excels as a poet of immense attention and vigor; the intricacies of his subjects, their layered natures, are eloquently sung in poems of immeasurable beauty and conviction.

BLACK RIVER

"The black soot that we experienced in Port Harcourt in the last seven to eight years now, it's been constant, twenty-four hours of the day every day, for at least six to seven years apparently, and it means that every day residents of Port Harcourt have no option but to be inhaling this black soot on a daily basis—newborns, children under five, adults, men, women, elderly—everybody is made a smoker because of the exposure to the black soot."
— Dr. Bieye Briggs, Public Health Physician and Environmental Advocate

My mother stands motionless in the water,
        infested by oil, drowned in half—her black-colored

palms clasped together, whispering the
        language creamed w/ oil. We greet mornings from the height

of our raft & wake to sooty breakfasts
        with breaths of carbon. My uncle became breathless

upholding convulsion in the terra incognita
        of his body. Say our dead offered for revenue—

strategy for government—money w/ oil companies, money
        in the well of their pockets. Oil blooms, but happiness recedes;

dune to dust. I recall the violent motion
        of the woman next door after her newborn became

an addition to the legion of dead in this place
        & her husband still nurturing abnormalities in his

manhood. See, the water
levels again, the house falls to flood. Even the dead

are still searching for a home in the land
ravaged by water & black oil. The woman at the edge

of the interview holds on to her tears—
says: *I came to the camp handful with my son, but I'm leaving*

with hands empty of him—again, *I know the past belongs*
in the past, my son belonged to the past, but my grievances

belong to the future. The footbridge collapsed,
see how water beholds teeth. But life goes on, & we sail through it

with our grievances solemn like the paddle hitting
the face of the water.

EID AL-FITR IN ILORIN

after Romeo Oriogun

Again, the morning comes alive like a season
of harvest, of prayers. I unmask the day,
my mouth cascading clean waterfall with a bright-eyed
smile. Holiness dawns on me—& I
unbottle a single alhamdulillah like a fine stereo.

Today earth embodies the hallow—say, in one
of its most sacred forms. I break into force with
my brother, our bodies clothed with neatly
embroidered agbada like an oshibana,
holding on to prayer mats like weapons of war,

as if we were all compelled by a spell to hold
on to them. In our journey, there is no loud music
blaring in the distance—the road pervaded with
an army of new clothes. On the other side of the road,
a group of men, in sections, chant the glory of Eid—

others beating the life of the bandiri drum,
the kind that needs the bare wideness of the palm.
Closer to Unity Rd., on this day, the road becomes
a haven of God—a place to whittle your grievances

to the all-encompassing, igniting your prayers
with big old radios bursting waves
as sounds placed closely to their prayer mats,
transmitting the soul of the muezzin's voice with
cracks. Say a fragment of nomads forfeited their

journey of movement & listened to the cracking
voice of Eid from their abode of withdrawal.

With my brother, & other unknown itinerants,
we do not raise the white flag of surrender; we seek
the heart of the prayer ground, which means we do
not capitulate the haven of our dreams. Seeking the light,
I have learned about light, but I do not mean
photons, I mean the sweet voice of God that dawns on
us in the flesh of the Imams.

On the way home, we gather our grief
like a mother gathering everything important to her,
the shadows of our sins flung into our breast pocket.
Say we've embraced once again the ripple we toppled
away when we trekked toward the paradise of Eid.
Say we do not return through the path that brought us there,
like a colony of ants returning from exile, we journeyed
embracing the misdeed we left behind. There is enough
ripped faith waiting for us at home.

IN ANOTHER WORLD OF LIVING

fire dies in your throat
a god relinquishing the light of what you seek
haven of bloated miracles
a room embroidered with chandeliers
& oshibanas where loneliness is a faraway thing
like your father
like your mother's elation
nightmare stills in your dreams filled with bones
dusty bones
napalm-ridden cities grown inside
the belly of your sleep
jubilance eludes you
in every universe
you an alien in a world of elation
it is so easy to think about love
when you are wrecked with loneliness
like the kettles abandoned behind a rural mosque
seeking your lover's hands & water
& you have not learned to avoid a variety of things
the blueness of a body
the sinkhole for your balanced rhythm
the diorama of your dreams designed with cadavers
in another world of living
you thrive on the mention of your anxieties
filling every doing with the bubbles of water
the first time you loved a woman
you crushed the hypothesis of fear
built on the quicksand of your mind
say you are afraid of a confession that pulls you into a body of water
here there is a dream floating away

INTERSECTIONS

"Renowned gospel singer, Tope Alabi, has responded to the controversy arising from the lyrics of her song. The singer in a viral video was seen singing in Yoruba, using the phrase 'Aboru Aboye,' a greeting common among traditionalists (Ifa initiates)."
—The Guardian (Nigeria)

"'Aboru Aboye' is purely Yoruba language, not for Ifa priests."
—Tope Alabi

At the mention of faith, words split between opposites,
glistening like a broken mirror
flipped into the fire. A quilt, ascribed to a mattress—
lay it on this bed & never another.

This word is a man sitting in the deep filth
of convention,
to push off the bridge of the hallow, into another.
Take a word for light, take it for darkness in another,
say you do not belong here,

language with stain. A steep edge between
two intersections of language.
An old bearded man in a white robe says, a ó rúbọ,
which means, we will sacrifice;
give to the Lord, what he owns.

In another, a man with a wide crucifix adorning his neck
repeats the same thing, a ó rúbọ,

which means, we will sacrifice;
give to the Lord, what he owns.
How the use of language can become a sacrilege
deep in the fiber of tongues.
See how words fall into the depths of discord.
Language is a genesis of identity.

CONFABULATION

There is no memory, only thorns.
Their sharp edges poking my desire

for a paternal reminiscence. I have
conjured confabulations through

the eyes of photographs, waded
through the tumult of recalling

& yet memory leaves me wanting,
the desire for tangible remembrances.

The world, a canopy of longing,
& this is no dream, only desire.

Once, memory granted me a line, but
everything would fit into my palm.

To remember the voice of the wind
is to forget the touch of the flame.

Forgetfulness, like effigies in the dark.
Forgetfulness, like a body losing its self;

the dawn of its leaving. I have
moved to the edge of auditory hallucination,

hearing a jumble of voices in the cenote of my head.
Because my memory begins at the end of everything.

ATAVISTIC VESTIGES AFTER THE RAIN

Salvador Dalí, 1939, oil on canvas

The cloud is a white smoke made of glasses,
the color of your father's death.

& twilight looms below God's brow
& the clouds rubble in the aftermath

of heaven mourning your loss with rain;
water drooling from God's eyes for the grief of this world,

& the world is a floating rock
punctured in difficult places by time—

held by the crutches of our remembrance;
the regurgitation of memories.

& the unearthing of forgetfulness
a civil war of the psyche.

Receding the footprints of a father & son
submerged in the sand dunes of disappearance—

faded memories immersed in some pathways,
withdrawing all vestiges of his existence,

but the gallery says forgetfulness is a liar,
& your mother's voice at the edge of tears.

In a dream, the memory is white as an albumen,
eroding every remembrance of the once was.

Forgetfulness is half-elegy—take father by the album
& whisper into his forgotten voice faded as dust.

You, a rock half-eaten by its hunting past.
In your last dream, your father held you by the palm
& strode into the bones he left behind.

I AM TETHERED TO POSSIBILITIES

On a Saturday, my mother
wraps blended beans
in a green leaf, her swift hands
like her mother's
& my brother laughs at the size
of my pap—& say àfi bí àlájà—
how food can be an eruption
of the dust in my memories.
Seven years before my brother
unfurled the phrase—it was
a night, & I mean the one with stars
in [ ] ~~absentee~~
where we sat behind a pot
the color of the night—
filled with moimoi—watching flies
dazzle around the LED bulb.
My grandmother hobbled—
her steps carried the weight
of decades of childbirth,
of child deaths, of laughter,
of seawater dribbled from the
universe of the retina. & she said:
ẹwọ ilé wá sùn—which means,
she beckoned us into the warmth
of our bed, which could mean,
we are the stars in her night sky.
Once, my mother smacked silence
onto my lips with her hefty palms
which uprooted my grandmother's

anger, she said: ọmọ dé là wọn ọmọ yi
which means we are little flowers
planted on their hands
by the Lord. I unearth her from
a photograph, & there's
laughter. I bite a smirk into my lips.
I still remember my dead beyond
grievances; the humorous memories,
another laugh splits from my lips
once again accompanied by a lonely tear.

PHONEMIC ANALYSIS

I kneel at the Calvary,
the sun pelting my skin like a rainstorm
of fragmented pieces of glass,
I drag myself toward a crucifix
where phonology says:
[a boy] —> [a broken boy] / [grief]—[grief]
I think myself a guitar's string
blessing the threnodies of the aches in this poem,
who will crush pomegranates
into juice for me?
Who will beat the bush of this boy into
a floral garden of roses?
Who will pour joy like a fricative sound
into the living of this boy?
I seek the rule to the deletion of grieving, where:
[grief] —> [deleted] / [bliss]—[bliss]
Where I will sleep through the night
without the body of a knife lurking in my dreams.
Where I will sleep through the night
without drowning in the pool of my own fears.
Where I will sleep through the night
& not wake up as a butterfly's wing.
But insertion says:
[insert] —> [grief] / [bliss]—[bliss]   of a boy.
Recently, I touch things & they flower out a
monochrome
of death & my father—how he squeezed life out of him
like an orange.
Dear poet, when will you stop performing an autopsy

with poems on all the broken things you know,
~~especially~~ including yourself?
This poem, a psych ward, this poem, a psych nurse
which grew   from your psyche.
Like a wood frog, I'm still holding my pee
through hours, through the night
where pain is a bagpiper blowing its pipe
to me in these times of war.

WHIFF

Tonight, the air is lenient.
I'm outside the door to the house
that is my mother's house, that is

outside the being of my living,
I mean, outside the confinement
of what my mind wants.

I stare up at the sky & there's
no moon except little stars twinkling
dull glimmers like my mother's

eyeballs. The welkin unearths
a door into other grievances—
the ones I cradle at every edge.

My mother smiles in her sleep
& I hold on to this memory, like a baby
in my arms. A woman illuminating

inside her grievances—tethered to the
harsh wind of life. A woman of substance
comes in a hailing literature; I say a woman

dumped by the shore from the teeth
of a storm. Another funeral reminds
me that my father did not become;

the halt of life that crushes a becoming.
& daily, my longing fastens to the emptiness
he left behind while every thought becomes

a poem inside the universe
of my body. See, drought begins
with the water, before the man,

before the rows of dry greens—set like
cornrows. Which is, the grievances
that made my father into an empty soprano,

before the wreckage of my mother's
youthfulness—before the foundry
that thaws my scrawny little bliss.

My friend thinks I'm guilty of holding on
too much to the past—like the man in Joseph-Désiré Court's
Scene of the Deluge—bloating the possibilities

of a luxurious future. Even at the end,
the inflated balloon bursts or floats away like
my father's breath. See, I want to revel

in all the booming glory of my grievances,
because the scenery of leaving does not elude me.
I'm still made of the whiff Pa left behind.

AUGUST THIRD

I let this day wash over me like a river of hot & cold
edging. Say my body
is the landscape, withholding the clash of waters on
its chest. & when I say it unfurls like laughter
-ridden mouth with long jutting canines.
I mean everything comes as a two-edged blade.
The paternal is celestial as a comet, life-wrenching
as lava & faceless as my father's name in my thoughts.
The maternal flip side—weightless with grief,
a pothole-free tarred surface, & a hallway sprinkled
with confetti. On days like this, I billow between the
spiky tongue of a cactus & Stevie Wonder's
"Happy Birthday." My father's music is a dead one,
& my mother's song is a hand unfettering the night
undoing sleep from my eyeballs. But I carry a menhir
& I'm drunk with anguish. Mother said my father
promised her big candles & a birthday
empty of a lifelong ache while he lay on the
hospital bed, but some promises are birds without wings.
On this day, I don't know what my lips taste of
but there is a foundry melting the delight on my chest.

WHEN YOUR MOTHER IS A BIRD WHICH ACCOMPANIED LOVE INTO EXILE

"Exile is the dying voice of a wounded angel."
—Romeo Oriogun

Some roads lead to regret. & your mother is a portrait
of this expression, the terror of gnashing teeth. She sought,
accompanied love into exile, & abandoned you & your brother
to live like orphans, to scrub the algae
on your own walls. She bloomed, & blossomed in the land
of another man. To go into exile is to disappear inside
a mist. On cold nights, when there was no mother to undo
your shivers with warm blankets & heated water,
you undid a crescendo of litanies like a wounded angel
seeking the dawn of a motherly coexistence—but your liturgies
were smoke blowing into exile. & on days when boys your age
ran into their mothers' rooms to unearth the grievances of their
bellies, you ran into the emptiness your mother left behind
before she dived into disappearance. To unspool a compendium
of hunger from the edge of your lips, you wound through
a storm heavy with insomnia. You were the mirror reflecting
the turbulence of your own—& brother's body &
you chased the chandelier of your life until you thawed
& poured into oblivion—without unfolding the evening
of your life into beautiful photographs. Loss is a door
to many types of regret; your mother sits at the apex of the first.

MY TROUBLE WITH LANGUAGE HAS EVERYTHING TO DO WITH EITHER BLOOD OR INHERITANCE

After Ayokunle Falomo

Or colonialism. Because the flame licks the tongue & everything.
Like a snake, it impersonates a worm, curls itself into my mouth.
Because I learned language before history, before the alternation
of everything I learned as a child.

In English class, a boy asks why oesophagus can be spelled without the first *o*
why honour & colour can be without the *u*,
why trousers are pants, why the lift in the hallway is also an elevator,
why a biscuit is also a cookie, why the toilet becomes a restroom
even without a bed, all within a language.

Because I speak the language of the people that god-ed the tongue
of my forefathers. My first failure with language was my voice,
then the alteration of words where torch & flashlight became
torchlight, where short & knicker became *short-knicker*,
through my mother's tongue growing from the sheaf of my mouth.

I speak their language, but I lack the accent.
Every time, your accent gives you away. & in an attempt to sound more British,
the lady next door says *fank you* in place of *thank you*,
but learning the language pulls you not into the colo(u)r.

Once again, a Nigerian is asked why he speaks English so well,
& he would break into sheaves on the edge of indifference.
But see, the body learns wetness from the dampness of the rain.

LOOSE

I have carried you for so long in the gullet of my songs,
the sad, solemn depth of its billowing echoes.

There is a ghost in existence that undoes you
in my remembrance—like a mirage, like the monochrome

in the parlor that nurtured my nibble feet into fully grown.
The first poem I wrote gravitated toward memories,

the fingers of longing that sought coexistence with a man.
I was a nineteen-year-old listening to the symphonies of beer bottles

& cigarettes fading into smoke—the call of ashes from ashtrays
dancing into the wind. There is so much pressure for a boy

whose [mother & father] —> [mother] / [death]—
I want the smoke to be my witness for these words, but the zephyr

swallowed—like the mouth of nothingness, which means:
[smoke] —> [disperse] / [zephyr]—

I watched the guesthouse trying to christen my innocence,
but I did not carry an urgency for the red world—I knew

the silence of my body, & I wanted it. I knew what lingered
in the dark, I knew the sphere of my wants.

The boy I worked alongside in Hawa called me soft—his teeth tore
the air with laughter. I folded my naivety with a cup of garri

& four dried kuli kuli—& the smoke altered the sweet scent of what
I hoarded in my mouth. I knew the taste of cigarettes without

smoking. I knew the smell of sex without experimenting
with its cosmos. & there was so much longing in the breeze

culled from the history of what whittled the moon inside
the tunnel of home—the autopsy of what killed the little dove

I saw inside my dreams. Here, I'm thinking about you—drenched under
the wet sky of thoughts, listening to the street.
The waning moon echoes its silence. Crushed leaves. The looseness of my body.

THE PERSISTENCE OF MEMORY

Salvador Dalí, 1931, oil on canvas

Twilight at the threshold of a dream,
or the shoreline of memories. Everything
I've known about time is all I've known—
its waning & all the fading solidity of what the
present holds—melting on the branch
of the dry olive tree, the fading yesteryear,
like candies melting in the sun.
The past is the wreckage of a certain once-was-
present, or a once sunny day metamorphosed
into a fog. The past at the climax of decay,
with tinges of remembrance—like the years by the
riverbank, by the mountains of my watered
reminiscence. Time thaws, but memories persist.
The past discolors & decays through—
a soldier of ants feasting on dead roaches.
In some moments, I'm a tiny fly on the wheel
of a ticktock, & in other moments, I am a body
slumped in the nightmare of a blanching
remembrance. I hang my silence inside the zephyr
while I'm deep inside a dream deteriorating;
a body like a wide mirror reflecting the alchemy
of the future, into the present, into the past.

PRONOUNCEMENT

At the pronouncement of his death, your body upheld
screams—dotted
with clots of denial, though preceded by a near-death silence,
because silence
too is a language that opens like a door to everything,
before the world went dark in your body.

Because you were too young for the weight of this loss,
a kind of sad music,
so loud that it deafens. You told me stories—the recurrent
days before
the world welcomed you back into its fingers—

eyes wide awake, *it's not your time to die*—the cosmos
whispered into your awakening.
& the grievance that incited itself in your body; the regurgitation
of memories dark as kohl
surging you into the turbulent edge of the world.

Dying, the loose end of a body owning the leaving of its edict
& there are many times a man
on the apex of the world is reduced to dust & to the world
says: give me this one & take this grief.
Because the body becomes dust and the soul becomes memory.

ELEGY

The guilt I carry after the trample
is heavy as retribution.
In this world, you are a slow song.
At the doorsill of dying,
you are an apprentice of the wind.
& I carry a mind, shivering like an earthquake.
The worry of guilt like the wind
inside a conjuror's chalice;
pushing me to the edge,
how I smashed you into nakedness—
how the history of an unknowing
trample began with my foot.
The girl on WhatsApp says,
you are just a delicacy for dinner,
but I know what in turn lies at the edge of grieving.
& what remains of you is the broken shell
& the disappearing slowness
of your body.
I say to the night, forgive my eagerness.
I say to the night, forgive my extreme eagerness.
& what I want of time: my feet,
two steps backward; this eagerness,
suppressed by time. & you slithering across
the surface with your mucus-like slime—
going home to the family
that came checking on your dried body hours
after the apocalypse of my foot on your shell.

AFTER MOVING

After Andrew Hemmert, after Romeo Oriogun

I brim with loneliness in this place like an overfilled jar,
embracing this silence of my body like the lone tree in the yard
of my new home. Its branches, thin with leaves
& scanty edges, with stones dwelling in its environs.
Its thin branches spread beyond the wall, seeking to fill
its loneliness, reaching out to the tree in the next
compound. The first week I got here,
an old man offered me the solace of a stranger,
the world was silent on his tongue & his voice resided
in the movement of his fingers. He wrote, on the paper,
"You can come here whenever you need to
uphold the silence of your body, while we stare into the sky
for birds chirping & chirping." How he offered me
a dance when he was bereft of music, a tape with ripped
speakers. The voice of my country was the genesis of it all,
its clarion call; the root of my moving. I am a stranger
in this city where home resides where my breath
is my only companion. My memories replay the shape of home
& this place where I've come offers me the shape of exile.
It is Ramadan, I bask in the delightful taste of
my own meal & the heavy weight of probability
that lies on my sahurs. The lady next door calls
on to my retraction with a dialogue, but I reject
the music of her calling. Which means, I find too much rhythm
in my ~~own~~ silence. Which means it's so easy to reside
in the sinkhole of anxieties, beyond the doorsill of extreme thoughts.
The night falls like a crown on the apex of the day
once more, & the MP3 booming in the
background becomes the extension of my voice.

ENCHANTED BEACH WITH THREE FLUID GRACES

Salvador Dalí, 1938, oil on canvas

All things begin from the spindle,
we say—life spun from graces.
I grew like rain from the rumbles of my parents'
cloud, a dark dawn, admitting growth.
In the beginning, I squeezed into existence with a head,
white, silhouette-like—formed from
the stomach of the hard earth on a farther
landscape; face formed in a hole, a body merging
into visibility. The last war of my body
was unscathed, admitting the shapes of various
dances. The second grace, where I am a boy seeking
existential relevance, my visage like a landscape,
a male equestrian with a body of dust
pursuing the horse of his identity—relevance-seeking.
The thread of my life, stretched to the doorsill
of disappearance, the length of my language
nearing a silence. I am the last body rhyming
with the earth—becoming more illusion than truth.
Holding on to the edge of my thread, bowing to the ache
of an empty body, my fingers grip the edge of my cloth.
Nature becomes a skull.

WHITE RIVER

white river blossomed   in my crotch
at the doorsill of what   makes a man a man

the new river in me arrived in days sometimes in clots
wetting its bank like a stain   drowned me into a primordial fear—

the assumption of an unknown ailment

the first day   I woke up to the clouds   scattered on my lap
unknown & sticky   & because I nurtured a crude ignorance
absence of a man   I'd run to
& tell of my newfound ailment
my mother was father   & I was the father of the house

& because my mother is also my mother

because the thought of telling was a war   a scare of ailment
because father became a primrose in a graveyard   at the end of the beginning

because it was the first time God visited me in my crotch
my friend in school said
                    I was becoming a man   while already living as a father for my
                                                                    my siblings
& the husband of my mother

PREMONITION

From the nucleus of his history, my father lived in a blue world
where the reeds were trails that led him to the water.

I learned about the clipped half of his own Genesis;
his masculine half that diminished while he was in bloom.

I think about the truths in stories, & the lies woven around them.
I think about the plights of a tongue & the autobiographies beneath it.

Like my grandfather, my father dissolved into an elegy while
I was still a lush threading a sapling.

I spent a night thinking about how to wade through the fog of this morrow,
the premonition that lies behind this door whose knob I held,

but I do not know. I hold on to survival in my soliloquies, like a dream
where figurines are promising a man a journey with the absence of an apocalypse.

NOTES

The statement by Dr. Bieye Briggs on page 11 is from Burna Boy's *The Black River: Whiskey Documentary*, 2022.

The title "My Trouble with Language Has Everything to Do with Either Blood or Inheritance" is a direct line taken from "Etymologicon" by Ayokunle Falomo, and the poem was also inspired by his poem "Shibboleth."

The poem "Whiff" alters a line of "Before the Dark" by Adedayo Agarau.

ACKNOWLEDGMENTS

Thanks to the editors of the following publications in which these poems, sometimes in different versions, first appeared:

Ake: "Premonition"
Isele Magazine: "Black River" and "I Am Tethered to Possibilities"
Mizna: "Eid al-Fitr in Ilorin"
POETRY: "Phonemic Analysis" and "Enchanted Beach with Three Fluid Graces"
Rat World Magazine: "Loose"
Poetry Wales: "August Third"
Rough Cut Press: "When Your Mother Is a Bird Which Accompanied Love into Exile"
Uncanny Magazine: "In Another World of Living"
Saltbush Review: "Whiff"